At The Table

- Telling Culinary Moments -

Peter C. Johnson, MD

At The Table

Second Edition

Peter C. Johnson, MD

ISBN– 978-1-4357-1746-6

Printed in the United States of America

Disclaimer: The images depicted in this book do not represent any particular persons or places. Comments or questions can be addressed to the author at pjohnson@scintellix.com.

Additional copies of this book may be purchased at:
http://www.lulu.com/content/2474191

Also by the author:
<u>The Surgeons Are Tied Up In The Operating Room</u>
http://www.lulu.com/content/2436310

At the Table is dedicated to the following:

My wonderful family: Karen, Caroline, Thomas and Elizabeth.

My mother Irene, my late father Richard and my siblings — Mary, Patrick, Monica, Margaret, Madonna and Martha (Kelly).

The exceptional owner (Barbara McKenna) and staff (including chef Chris O'Brien) of Hyeholde Restaurant in Coraopolis, PA (www.hyeholde.com) who let me experience a fine dining kitchen as a prep chef and who proved that even an old surgeon can be taught new tricks. While no one from Hyeholde was a model for the characters in this book, its excellent service, cuisine and ambience were clearly what led me to explore this display of what happens every day in the fine dining industry. I am grateful to all of them.

I also dedicate this book to all of the chefs and waitstaff worldwide who cater to our endless need for fine culinary stimulation.

"What Do You *Mean*, You Only Had *One*?"

"And How Would You Like That Cell Phone Prepared, Ma'am?"

"I Only Said I *COULD*!"

"Chef Has Hunted Down Just The Thing For Your Anniversary."

"I *Knew* I Shouldn't Have Ordered Such A Heavy Meal."

“Chef *Does* Have A Way With Presentation, Doesn’t He?”

"Just A Moment. I'm Checking The Menu."

"All Right — Whose Bright Idea Was 'Eel Night?'"

"My Wife Would KILL To Dine Here."

"Chef Is A Magician With A Whisk, Isn't He?"

"It's Feng Shui..."

"I Always Have This When I Come Here."

"There. He *SAID* It Was Hot....*Now* Are You Satisfied???"

“It *WAS* Souffle—But Then You Kept Talking And Talking...”

"Amazing How They Can Live Anywhere."

"We Had A Little Botulinum Scare At Lunch.
Thankfully *That's* Past Us."

"But We Heard That You Welcome Hungry Friends
At *ALL* Hours..."

"Garnish."

"It's Today's Special."

“Fruit Flies.”

"She's Just Shy."

"It's Almost 'Eden Fresh' Here, Don't You Think?"

"I'll Have Whatever He's Having."

"This Is The Best I've Eaten All Day.
How About You, Harry?"

"Was There A Problem With Your Meal?"

"You Look Ravishing Tonight, Sylvia."

"You Two Are Younger Than Me.
It's Not Right."

"Well, Enough About Us — How About You?"

"Yes, I AM Waiting For Someone — Could You Be He?"

"We Call It 'Chef Special.' It's Not For The Squeamish."

"And The Damages Come To….."

"I Slave Away All Night Back There
And You Two Just *Sit* Here."

"Chef Tells Me All We Have Left Are Airline Snacks."

"He Doesn't Drink But I Sure Do"

"That's A Good Beginning..."

Training The Sous Chef

"You Both Want the Shrimp Special???"

"I Forgot To Mention How Literally They Take Things Around Here."

"Chef's Practicing His Heimlich Hug Again."

"And Let's Alert The Sommelier, Shall We?"

"Yes, We're Sopping Wet, Yet We're Big Tippers."

"Here's To Dining Out Of Wedlock."

"Stand Back."

"OK — Now Put It Down And Then Move Away...
...*Reallllll Slowwww*."

"You Might Be Amused By Service Here, Edmund."

"Faster!"

"Chef Found Them In The Kitchen. They Grew On Us."

"Just Bones For Stock, Chef."

"We Know You Don't Allow Pets But He's Family."

"One Sip Of Wine And POOF—He Was Gone."

“There — *THAT* French Enough For You?”

"Chef Just Goes Soft In The Presence Of Sturgeon."

"What Time Do You Get Off Tonight?"

"OK Folks, Dig In."

"Give Us A Moment. We're Celebrating 35 Long Years."

"Not Now, Chef—I'm Pouring."

"Let's Just Share The Next One, Shall We?"

"Man Over There Sent This To The Lady."

"Squid As Long As Your Leg — No Lie!"

Garde Manger

"Please Philip. For Once, *No* Chicken Wings."

"I Get *Real* Angry When My Drink Is Delayed."

"For The Life Of Me, I Don't Understand Why We're Out On A Weeknight."

"Should I be Worried That You Are Nice To Me But Rude To The Waiter?"

"After Moments Like This
A Real Calm Comes Over The Kitchen."

"Don't Fret—I'll Text Him."

"They're Right — It IS Still Breathing."

"To Us."

Chef's Day Off

“We’re Stackers.”

"Chef—The Stock Is Acting Up Again!"

"The Appetizers Here Are Certainly Generous, Aren't They?"

"The Other Nine Were Lost To The Kitchen Staff, I'm Afraid."

"This Isn't A Tipping Country, Is It?"

Chef, Hunting The Wild Morel.

"He Said 'Damn The Tip—Finish Your Peas.'"

"It's The Old Cold Water Trick."

"See—Popcorn Shrimp *Can* Be A Delicacy!"

"Amazing Illusion Martha —
When I look Through These Tines It's As If You're In Prison."

"Do You Have Handicapped Seating?"

"This Is My First Date — Is This Normal?"

Chef's Annual Meeting With The Owner

"Bill— 'Relax While I Get Your Drinks' Is Just A Figure Of Speech."

"Charlie — This *Isn't* Raffle's Long Bar, You Know."

"And A Little Arsenic For You, Mrs. Roach."

"It's My Son Aloysius. His Mom And I Thought You Might Like To Bring Him On, Out Back."

"Still Working On Yours, Ma'am?"

"She's Mine—NO! She's Mine!"

"One Potato, Two Potato, Three Potato, Four.
Will That Be All, Mr. Milner?"

"And If That Special Didn't Thrill You,
Wait Until You Hear This One!"

"Might I Join You For A Little Aperitif?"

"What's *Good???*"

"Yes, I'll Admit — Our Menu *IS* A Bit Forward-Looking."

"Dinner Is Served."

"We're Closed And I'm Just The Janitor.
But Order Whatever You Like
— I'm Having The Time Of My Life."

"Let's NOT Water Them Down This Time
And Just See What Happens."

“They’re Truffles. *Promise*.”

"Can You Hold Still For A Moment? He's A Cartoonist."

www.ingramcontent.com/pod-product-compliance
Ingram Content Group UK Ltd.
Pitfield, Milton Keynes, MK11 3LW, UK
UKHW051128260726
13967UKWH00010B/2929

9 781435 717466